FROM:

Prayers from the heart

Written and compiled by
Conover Swofford

Illustrated by Jane Eyre

Inspire Books in an imprint of
Peter Pauper Press, Inc.

Designed by Arlene Greco

For permissions please see
the last page of this book.

Visit us at www.peterpauper.com

Prayers from the heart

prayer is the soul's sincere desire,
  Uttered or unexpressed;
The motion of a hidden fire
That trembles in the breast.

JAMES MONTGOMERY

this is my daily prayer,
God bless you, go with God, . . .
thru all eternity,
My prayer will always be,
May you go with God.

WARREN ROBERTS

As we journey through life
side by side, hand in hand,
and heart to heart, we pray,
O Lord, that You will keep
our union sweet, steadfast,
and overflowing with love for
each other and You.

People who pray together
stay together.

pray without ceasing.

1 THESSALONIANS 5:17 NKJV

prayer is a sincere, sensible,
affectionate pouring out
of the soul to God, through
Christ in the strength and
assistance of the Spirit,
for such things as God
has promised.

JOHN BUNYAN

the more I pray for you,
the more God pours
His love through my heart
to you.

the prayer of a godly person
is powerful.

JAMES 5:16 NIRV

help me, O Lord, to be
more loving. . . . Help me
by my love to be the
witness of your love.

ALAN PATON

We are all works in progress and prayer is what keeps us in touch with our Maker's design for us.

As soon as we are with God
in faith and in love,
we are in prayer.

FRANÇOIS FÉNELON

thrice blest whose lives
are faithful prayers.

ALFRED, LORD TENNYSON

he shall pray to God,
and He will delight in him,
He shall see His face with joy,
For He restores to man His
righteousness.

JOB 33:26 KJV

[t]he prayer of the upright
is His delight.

PROVERBS 15:8 NKJV

We pray to find God's will
for us, not to nag Him into
letting us have our own way.

may the Lord watch
between you and me,
when we are parted from
each other's sight.

GENESIS 31:49 NEB

that you may know the
true love of God shining
forth to you in the love
of a friend—this is
my prayer.

We are God's gift to
each other. We should live
so that our entire lives are a
hymn of praise to God.

to pray is to know
the delight of seeing the
invisible God.

thanks be to God for
His indescribable gift!

2 CORINTHIANS 9:15 NKJV

praying puts us into
the heart of God and opens
our hearts to Him.

Let my prayer be set before
You as incense . . .

PSALMS 141:2 KJV

Your cares are my cares;
your hurts are my hurts;
your burdens are my burdens;
and together we can lay them
all at the Father's feet.

prayer is love raised to its
greatest power . . .

Robert J. McCracken

It is love that asks, that seeks,
that knocks, that finds, and
that is faithful to what it finds.

St. Augustine

prayer is love
in action.

Call to Me, and I will answer you,
and show you great and mighty
things, which you do not know.

JEREMIAH 33:3 KJV

therefore I say unto you,
What things soever ye desire,
when ye pray, believe that
ye receive them, and ye
shall have them.

MARK 11:24 KJV

Lord, help me live from day to day
In such a self-forgetful way,
That even when I kneel to pray
My prayer shall be for Others.

CHARLES DELUCENA MEIGS

I cannot think of a better way
Of showing you my love
Than by keeping you
constantly in prayer
Before God's throne above.

O, Sovereign Lord,
you are God! Your words are
trustworthy, and you have
promised these good things
to your servant.

2 SAMUEL 7:28 NIV

God grant that I may speak
according to his will, and
that my own thoughts may
be worthy of his gifts . . .

WISDOM OF SOLOMON 7:15 NEB

I tell you that if two of you on earth agree about anything you ask for, it will be done for you by my Father in heaven.

MATTHEW 18:19 NIV

f or where two or three
come together in my name,
there am I with them.

MATTHEW 18:20 NIV

prayer is the key
to the will of God.

But when you pray, go into a
room by yourself, shut the door,
and pray to your Father who is
there in the secret place . . .

MATTHEW 6:6 NEB

he prayeth best, who loveth best,
All things both great and small;
For the dear God who loveth us,
He made and loveth all.

SAMUEL TAYLOR COLERIDGE

God hears the slightest
whisper in my heart.

as long as there are tests,
there will be prayers in schools.

prayer is not to give us
control of God but to give
God control of us. It is not
to get God to work for us
but to allow God to
work through us.

You are my North Star, God—
constant,
bright,
enduring.
I take my direction
from You.

May you live the life and
know the love that God
intended for you when God
first thought of your creation
and spoke you into being.

And this is the confidence
that we have in him, that, if
we ask any thing according to
his will, he heareth us.

1 JOHN 5:14 KJV

When we send our prayers
up to God, He sends back
His love and care.

Some people pray at certain times,
    While others pray all day.
    God made us individuals,
    But asks each one to pray.

L ORD, lift up the light of
Your countenance upon us.
You have put gladness
in my heart.

PSALMS 4:6-7 NKJV

prayer is what keeps
our faith moving along the
pathway to Heaven.

Ah, Sovereign LORD, you
have made the heavens and
the earth by your great power
and outstretched arm.
Nothing is too hard for you.

JEREMIAH 32:17 NIV

In the presence of love and
the presence of prayer is the
presence of God.

Prayer is the action of our
heart that lifts our loved ones
into the presence of God.

Constant prayer
is constant love.

I will praise You, O Lord,
with my whole heart . . .

PSALMS 9:1 AMP

I leave my prayers with
Him alone
Whose will is wiser
than my own.

ELIZA M. HICKOK

prayer is the greatest unused
power in the world . . .

ROGER BABSON

It is not so much the words
that we speak but the feeling
down deep in our hearts that
is our prayer to God.

father, help me to live
so that my prayers are
reflected in my
everyday life.

then you will call upon me
and come and pray to me,
and I will listen to you. You
will seek me and find me
when you seek me with
all your heart.

JEREMIAH 29:12-13 NIV

But I have prayed for thee,
that thy faith fail not . . .

may all the blessings
God has to give be
bestowed on you.

Every good and precious gift
Comes down from God above.
He gives us many wonderful things
And the greatest of these is LOVE.

I pray also for those who
will believe in me . . . ,
that all of them may be one,
Father, just as you are in
me and I am in you.

JOHN 17:20-21 NIV

Sweet hour of prayer!
sweet hour of prayer!
That calls me from a world of care,
And bids me at my Father's throne
Make all my wants and
wishes known . . .

W. W. WALFORD

there's a garden where
Jesus is waiting,
There's a place that is
wondrously fair;
For it glows with the light
of His presence,
'Tis the beautiful garden
of prayer.

ELEANOR ALLEN SCROLL

prayer is not just
talking to God—
it is listening to
His reply.

When you have prayed about
your problem and turned it
over to God, don't try to
snatch it back again.

When you come to
the end of your rope, tie a
prayer knot, and hang on.

W. T. McLean